AuthorHouse™
1663 Liberty Drive
Bloomington, IN 47403
www.authorhouse.com
Phone: 1 (800) 839-8640

Published by AuthorHouse 09/21/2018

ISBN: 978-1-5462-5740-0 (sc)
978-1-5462-5739-4 (e)

Library of Congress Control Number: 2018910122

Print information available on the last page.

author**HOUSE**®

Find Ginger

RORIE CAPARELLI

Hi everyone. My name is Ginger and I am a 6 year old Pomeranian. I was rescued by my family from the Westchester SPCA. I had been transferred there from another shelter in North Carolina for the big adoption event. I now have a mommy and daddy, two brothers, and a sister and feel so lucky to have found a home and a family to love.

I love being with my new family, but, when all the kids go off to school for the day, and I have the house to myself, I have to find comfortable places to hang on my own.

Photo by Caryn Posnansky at Caryn Leigh Photography

When I am all alone
In my cozy home,
I find the perfect place
to rest my face.
Let's Play Find Ginger

I am in a doll bed what do you think?
Girls love to be surrounded by pink.

Do you spot my head
in this crowded bed?

Can you see my back?
(It's near something black)

Where am I now? Do you have a hunch?
I'm just as furry as the rest of the bunch.

Can you find my shiny eyes,
When I'm among all of these guys?

How can this be?
I'm one of three!
Can you tell which one is me?

Wherever there's monkeys, penguins, leopards and bears,
You can be sure I will be there.

This one will trick you...
If you find me, I'll lick you!

I'm in the bed
Behind something red

Can you see me now
Next to the cow?

I'm sitting up
Between a bear and a pup.

Can you find my face,
In this busy place?

Even I can't find me here. Oh dear!

That's not me!
Look for my eyes
I'm behind the pillow. Surprise!

It's quiet at night,
And I'm out of sight.

Can you see my ear
Next to a bear?

I love to hide
With a frog near my side.

Is there any doubt
Where I'm resting my snout?

I'm on someone's head
in my sister's bed.

I'm on top of the group
near a giant pink poop.

Do you want to laugh?
I'm above a giraffe.

Can you see me asleep
On top of the heap?

It's quiet and dark
You won't hear me bark.

Isn't this funny?
I'm close to a bunny.

It's so crowded in here.
Can you spot my ear?

Don't make a mistake!
I'm near a green snake.

Keep trying, don't fail.
Just look for my tail.

I'm somewhere in this pile,
But close to a smile....

See my pretty hair?
I'm hiding under a chair.

Do you see my nose
Among the clothes?

Don't I look sweet, in my doggy car seat?
On our way home from buying some treats.
Whether in bed or on the floor,
Ginger is going to hide some more.
Find Ginger!

Printed in the United States
By Bookmasters